HOLIDAY COOKIES
RECIPES FOR JOLLY GOOD TREATS

table of contents

basic sugar cookie dough

MAKES: ABOUT 24 COOKIES | PREP TIME: 30–40 MINUTES | BAKE TIME: 10–12 MINUTES PER BATCH

This master recipe makes sugar cookie dough that's strong enough for little hands to roll, sculpt, and cut with cookie cutters. Plus, it's versatile and can be turned into all the playful sugar cookies found in this book. *Note: Make the dough one day ahead of time since it needs to sit in the refrigerator overnight.*

INGREDIENTS

- ❏ 1 cup unsalted butter, softened
- ❏ ¾ cup sugar
- ❏ 1 large egg
- ❏ 1 teaspoon vanilla extract or
   ½ teaspoon of lemon or almond extract
- ❏ ¼ teaspoon salt
- ❏ 2½ cups flour

1. Using an electric mixer at medium-high speed, cream the butter, gradually adding the sugar. Beat in the egg until evenly mixed, then blend in the vanilla (or lemon or almond extract), and salt.

2. With a wooden spoon, stir the flour into the creamed ingredients, about one third at a time, until evenly blended. The dough may seem soft, but it will firm up when refrigerated.

3. Divide the dough in half. Flatten each portion into a disk about ¾-inch thick and seal in plastic wrap. Refrigerate overnight.

4. The next day, remove the dough from the refrigerator and let it warm up for about 10 minutes (30 minutes for the Pinwheel Pops on page 5). Preheat the oven to 375°. Roll the dough to a ¼-inch thickness between two pieces of waxed paper or plastic wrap lightly dusted with flour. Make any of the cookies on the following pages (pages 3-9) according to their directions.

5. When they're ready to bake, place the cookies on a sturdy, ungreased cookie sheet and bake for 10 to 12 minutes, or until the cookies start to brown lightly around the edges. Let the cookies cool for 5 minutes on the sheet before transferring them to a cooling rack. Frost and decorate the cookies after they have cooled completely.

cookie frosting

MAKES: 1 CUP | PREP TIME: 20 MINUTES

This basic frosting can be spread with a knife or squeezed through a pastry bag (or a sealable plastic bag with a snip cut out of one corner) onto sugar cookies. If you plan to pipe the frosting through a bag, make it stiffer by adding a little less milk.

INGREDIENTS

- ❏ 2 cups confectioners' sugar, sifted
- ❏ ¼ cup unsalted butter, softened
- ❏ ½ teaspoon vanilla extract
- ❏ 1 to 2 tablespoons milk
- ❏ Liquid or paste food coloring (optional)

1. In a small bowl, and using an electric mixer set at low speed, beat the confectioners' sugar, butter, and vanilla extract until combined.

2. Mix in 1 tablespoon of milk and, if necessary, continue adding milk or confectioners' sugar until it reaches spreading consistency. If desired, stir in the food coloring until blended.

frosty snowmen

MAKES: 2 DOZEN | PREP TIME: 1 HOUR | BAKE TIME: 10–12 MINUTES PER BATCH

The secret to these sweet snowmen is their scarves—they're cut out of fruit leather.

INGREDIENTS

- ❑ Basic Sugar Cookie Dough (see page 2)
- ❑ Snowman cookie cutter or card stock template
- ❑ Frosting, white
- ❑ Gumdrops and M&M's Minis
- ❑ Shredded coconut
- ❑ Fruit leather or shoestring licorice

1. Roll out the dough and use a cookie cutter, or your template and a knife (adults only), to cut out the snowmen. Bake as directed in the dough recipe on page 2.

2. Once cooled, frost the cookies and add candy features and coconut snow. To form two scarves, cut a 7-inch piece of fruit leather in half lengthwise and notch the ends (or use licorice). Tie the scarf around the snowman's neck.

rudolph the red-nosed cookie

MAKES: ABOUT 24 COOKIES | PREP TIME: 1 HOUR | BAKE TIME: 12 MINUTES PER BATCH

A plate of these reindeer cookies and a glass of milk will make Santa merry on Christmas Eve.

INGREDIENTS

- ❑ Basic Sugar Cookie Dough, plain (see page 2) or chocolate (see box below)
- ❑ 3-inch-long card stock template for Rudolph's head
- ❑ Knot-shaped pretzels
- ❑ Frosting, white or chocolate
- ❑ M&M's
- ❑ Red gumdrops or Red Hots

1. Roll out the cookie dough and set your template on the dough. With the point of a sharp knife (adults only), cut out the reindeer heads. Bake as directed in the dough recipe on page 2.

2. Let cool. Break apart the pretzels to form antlers and attach them at the top of the reindeer's head with dabs of frosting. Add M&M eyes and a red candy nose.

> **Chocolate Sugar Cookies:**
> To make the Basic Sugar Cookie Dough chocolate-flavored, mix in ½ cup of unsweetened cocoa powder before the last third of flour is added to the dough.

striped mittens

MAKES: 2 DOZEN | PREP TIME: 45 MINUTES | CHILL TIME: 1 HOUR | BAKE TIME: 10–12 MINUTES

Warm up on a December night with edible mittens and a cup of hot cocoa.

1. Prepare the sugar cookie dough on page 2. Halve the dough and color each portion with **food coloring**. Flatten both portions into ½-inch-thick rectangles, wrap them in plastic, and refrigerate until firm, about 30 minutes.

2. Atop plastic wrap, use a lightly floured rolling pin to roll out each dough portion into an 8- by 12-inch rectangle. Layer the rectangles, then rewrap the dough in plastic and refrigerate for 30 minutes.

3. Use a long, sharp knife to halve the dough crosswise. Stack the pieces, then slice the dough into ¼-inch-wide strips. On plastic wrap, lay the strips on their side, stripes facing up, alternating colors. Press the strips together. Cover the dough with another sheet of plastic wrap and gently flatten the dough with a rolling pin to adhere the strips. Remove the wrap. Use cookie cutters to form the mittens, then bake according to directions on page 2.

4. If you like, use a straw to poke a hole in each mitten cookie immediately after baking. Tie pairs together with a length of **licorice lace**.

candy cane twists

MAKES: 18 | PREP TIME: 45 MINUTES | CHILL TIME: 30 MINUTES | BAKE TIME: 10–12 MINUTES

Peppermint extract adds that authentic candy cane flavor to these colorful treats.

1. Prepare the sugar cookie dough on page 2. Mix 1 teaspoon **peppermint extract** and ½ teaspoon **vanilla extract** into the prepared dough, then divide it into thirds. Dye one third with ½ teaspoon **red food coloring** and another with ½ teaspoon **green food coloring**. Flatten each third into a ½-inch thick rectangle, wrap it in plastic, and refrigerate until firm, about 30 minutes.

2. On a lightly floured surface, roll a pair of tablespoon-size pieces of contrasting colored dough into 8-inch-long ropes. Twist them together, pinch the ends, then bend the cookies into a candy cane shape. Repeat with the remaining dough and bake according to directions on page 2.

pinwheel pops

MAKES: 24 | PREP TIME: 45 MINUTES | CHILL TIME: 90 MINUTES | BAKE TIME: 13 MINUTES

Enjoy these cookie pops with their swirls of light and dark doughs.

1. Prepare the sugar cookie dough on page 2. Halve the dough. Mix 1 ounce melted and slightly cooled **unsweetened chocolate** into one half. Flatten both halves into ½-inch-thick rectangles, wrap them in plastic, and refrigerate until firm, about 30 minutes.

2. Atop plastic wrap, use a lightly floured rolling pin to roll out each half of the dough into an 8- by 12-inch rectangle. Lay the plain dough on top of the chocolate. Starting with a long side, tightly roll the dough into a log. Wrap it in plastic and refrigerate it for 1 hour.

3. Slice the roll into ½-inch-thick rounds. Shape each round into a circle, then insert a lollipop stick 1 inch deep into each cookie and bake according to directions on page 2.

cookie carolers

MAKES: 2 DOZEN | PREP TIME: 45 MINUTES | BAKE TIME: 10–12 MINUTES

Serve these sweet songsters as a treat after caroling.

1. Prepare the sugar cookie dough on page 2. Cut out rounds of cookie dough. Using a chopstick or straw, poke a hole in the center of each cookie and wiggle it to make a wide open mouth.

2. Bake according to the baking instructions on page 2. Re-poke the holes.

3. Once cooled, use icing to pipe on hair, eyes, and lips.

windows and doors

MAKES: 12–14 COOKIES | PREP TIME: 60 MINUTES | BAKE TIME: 10–12 MINUTES

Deck the halls with these edible ornaments.

1. Prepare the sugar cookie dough on page 2. Cut out rectangles (3 by 4 inches for windows, 2½ by 4½ inches for doors). If the dough gets too soft to handle, slide the waxed paper and dough onto a third (ungreased) baking sheet and refrigerate for 10 minutes.

2. Arrange the prepared cookies on the baking sheets, leaving about 1 inch between them. To make cookie ornaments, use a straw to cut holes at the tops.

3. Bake according to the baking instructions on page 2. Once cooled, your child can frost the windows and doors then add details: candy cane candles, gumdrop doorknobs, gummy ring wreaths, or anything you may dream up! Store the decorated cookies in an airtight container.

TIP: On flour-dusted waxed paper, roll out the dough starting in the middle and working out toward the edges.

TIP: For cookie ornaments, cut holes in the tops of the dough rectangles with a straw before baking. Once the cookies cool, tie on ribbon hangers.

christmas tree pops

MAKES: 5 DOZEN | **PREP TIME:** 45 MINUTES | **BAKE TIME:** 10–12 MINUTES

Decorating Christmas tree pops will keep the little elves in your family busy.

1. Prepare the sugar cookie dough on page 2. Cut the cookie dough into 3¼-inch-tall triangles.

2. Place on the prepared cookie sheets. Insert a craft stick three quarters of the way under each cookie.

3. Bake according to the baking instructions on page 2. Once cool, decorate with piped-on icing and candy "lights."

kris kringle cookies

MAKES: 12–18 COOKIES | **PREP TIME:** 45 MINUTES | **BAKE TIME:** 10–12 MINUTES

Invite Saint Nick to make a cameo appearance in your holiday cookie baking this season.

1. Prepare the sugar cookie dough on page 2. Cut out the cookie dough using a heart-shaped cookie cutter and bake according to the baking instructions on page 2.

2. Once cooled, turn each heart upside down and frost the rounded parts with white icing. Then top with shredded coconut to create Santa's beard. Use red decorating gel to turn the point of the heart into Santa's hat and add more coconut for the trim. Add mini chocolate-chip eyes and a red gel nose.

spice up your sugar cookies

These three decorating ideas transform basic cookies into oooh-and-aaaah-worthy edibles.

1. Egg Yolk Paint

For each color, add 4 drops of food coloring to an egg yolk and mix well. Use a clean paintbrush to create a design, then bake the cookies according to your recipe.

2. Mini-Marshmallow Masterpieces

Use clean scissors or kitchen shears to cut mini marshmallows in half. If you like, dip the sticky side of the marshmallow in colored sugar. Use the pieces to create poinsettias, snowmen, and more.

3. Icing Swirls

Frost a cookie with a base color. Before it sets, pipe on rows of other colors of frosting. Run a toothpick through the colors in evenly spaced lines to blend and create swirls.

stained glass candy cookies

MAKES: 3 DOZEN | PREP TIME: 45 MINUTES | BAKE TIME: 10 MINUTES PER BATCH

Fill your cookies with multicolored windows, all made out of crushed candies.

YOU WILL NEED

- ❏ Heavy-duty aluminum foil
- ❏ Nonstick cooking spray
- ❏ Basic Sugar Cookie Dough (see page 2)
- ❏ Round cookie cutters and aspic cutters
- ❏ Chopstick or straw
- ❏ Crushed hard candies
- ❏ Shoestring licorice or ribbon (optional)

1. Cover your baking sheet with the foil and lightly coat with cooking spray. Roll out the dough and cut out rounds. Use aspic cutters to cut out shapes within each circle. To make a hanging cookie, punch a hole in the top of each cookie with a chopstick.

2. Place on the baking sheet and bake as directed (see page 2). Halfway through the baking time, fill the holes with the crushed candy (do not overfill). Once thoroughly baked, repoke the hole at the top of the cookie.

3. Cool, then thread with shoestring licorice or ribbon.

ice-cream treewiches

MAKES: 12 | PREP TIME: 15 MINUTES | BAKE TIME: 10 MINUTES

These frosty-cool cookie treats are sure to bring warm smiles to some happy kids!

YOU WILL NEED

- ❏ Christmas tree cookie cutter
- ❏ Basic Sugar Cookie Dough (see page 2), colored green
- ❏ Candy "ornaments"
- ❏ White Frosting
- ❏ Half-gallon block of ice cream

1. Cut out trees from the dough and bake as directed.

2. Once cooled, attach the candy with icing to half of the trees.

3. Cut a ½-inch-thick slice off the ice-cream block and cut out an ice cream tree with the cookie cutter.

4. Sandwich the ice-cream trees between the cookies, wrap in plastic, and freeze.

chocolate crinkles

MAKES: 3 DOZEN | **PREP TIME:** 20 MINUTES | **CHILL TIME:** 2 HOURS
BAKE TIME: 10 MINUTES PER BATCH

Beneath the crackled, powdery surface of these cookie-brownie hybrids is a soft interior that tastes like a fresh chocolate doughnut.

INGREDIENTS

- ❑ ¾ cup butter, melted
- ❑ ½ cup unsweetened cocoa powder
- ❑ 1 cup sugar
- ❑ 2 eggs
- ❑ 2 teaspoons vanilla extract
- ❑ 2 cups flour
- ❑ 1 teaspoon baking powder
- ❑ 1 teaspoon baking soda
- ❑ ½ teaspoon salt
- ❑ 6 ounces mini semisweet chocolate chips (about 1¼ cups)
- ❑ ¾ cup confectioners' sugar

1. In a large bowl, stir together the melted butter, cocoa powder, and sugar. Whisk in the eggs and vanilla extract. In a medium bowl, stir together the flour, baking powder, baking soda, and salt. Using a large spoon, slowly add the dry ingredients to the chocolate mixture. Stir in the chips. Refrigerate the dough for 2 hours.

2. Heat the oven to 350°. Form the dough into 1-inch balls, then roll them in confectioners' sugar. Bake the cookies on an ungreased baking sheet for 10 minutes. Set the baking sheet on a wire rack for 5 minutes, then lightly dust the cookies with the remaining confectioners' sugar. Transfer the cookies directly onto the rack to cool thoroughly.

marbled chocolate-chip oatmeal cookies

MAKES: 2 DOZEN | **PREP TIME:** 20 MINUTES | **CHILL TIME:** 2 HOURS | **BAKE TIME:** 10-11 MINUTES PER BATCH

Not that you need a reason to bake cookies, but this recipe puts the good-for-you grain into delicious treats for kids of all ages.

INGREDIENTS

- ❑ 1 cup (2 sticks) butter or margarine, softened
- ❑ 1 cup sugar
- ❑ ½ cup brown sugar, firmly packed
- ❑ 2 eggs
- ❑ 1½ teaspoons vanilla extract
- ❑ 2 cups plus 2 tablespoons all-purpose flour
- ❑ 1 teaspoon baking soda
- ❑ ½ teaspoon salt
- ❑ ¼ cup baking cocoa
- ❑ 1 cup oats (quick or old-fashioned, uncooked), divided
- ❑ 1 cup semisweet chocolate morsels, divided

1. In a large bowl, beat the butter and sugars until creamy. Add the eggs and vanilla extract and beat well.

2. In a separate bowl, combine 2 cups of the flour, the baking soda, and the salt, mixing well. Stir the dry mixture into the batter.

3. Divide the dough evenly between 2 bowls. Mix the baking cocoa into one batch and the remaining 2 tablespoons of flour into the other. Stir ½ cup of oats and ½ cup of chocolate morsels into each batch, then cover and chill both doughs 2 hours or overnight.

4. Heat the oven to 375°. To shape the cookies, combine 1 tablespoon of each dough into a golf-ball–size ball, twisting or smooshing the doughs together (a great step for kids!). Place the balls 2 inches apart on an ungreased cookie sheet and bake 10 to 11 minutes or until the light-colored dough is golden brown.

5. Allow the cookies to cool 2 minutes on the cookie sheet, then transfer them to wire racks to cool completely. Store leftovers in a tightly covered container.

caramel thumbprints

MAKES: 26 COOKIES | PREP TIME: 40 MINUTES | BAKE TIME: 10, 4 MINUTES PER BATCH

Melted caramel candy adds luscious richness to the cocoa goodness of these cookies.

INGREDIENTS

- ❏ 1½ cups flour
- ❏ ½ cup cocoa powder
- ❏ ¼ teaspoon salt
- ❏ ¼ teaspoon baking powder
- ❏ ½ cup unsalted butter, softened
- ❏ ⅔ cup brown sugar, packed
- ❏ 1 large egg, separated
- ❏ 3 tablespoons milk
- ❏ 1 teaspoon vanilla extract
- ❏ 1 cup finely chopped pecans
- ❏ 26 chocolate-covered caramel candies, such as Dove or Rolo

1. In a medium bowl, sift together the flour, cocoa powder, salt, and baking powder and set aside.

2. Using an electric mixer set on medium-high speed, cream the butter and sugar until fluffy, about 3 minutes. Add the egg yolk, milk, and vanilla and mix until blended, about 1 minute. Add the flour mixture in two batches and beat until combined, about 1 minute. Cover the bowl with plastic wrap and refrigerate the dough for 30 minutes.

3. Heat the oven to 350°. Line a cookie sheet with parchment paper. In a medium bowl, beat the egg white with a fork. Set aside about ¼ cup of the pecans; put the rest on a plate. Roll 1 tablespoon of the dough into a ball, coat it with egg white, and roll it in the nuts. Repeat with the remaining dough. Put the cookies on the sheet, leaving about 3 inches between them. With your thumb, make an indentation in the center of each cookie, then reshape the outside edges, if they crack.

4. Bake the cookies for 10 minutes, then take them from the oven and gently press a caramel candy into each cookie. Bake until the chocolate and caramel soften, about 4 minutes. Grease the tines of a fork with butter and press on each candy to flatten it slightly. Sprinkle on the reserved nuts, then cool the cookies on a rack.

chocolate surprises

MAKES: 20 COOKIES | PREP TIME: 25 MINUTES | BAKE TIME: 10, 4 MINUTES PER BATCH

Think of these cookies as miniature holiday gifts for family and friends—beautiful on the outside with a special surprise inside: a gooey marshmallow center.

INGREDIENTS

Cookies:
- ❏ 2 cups flour
- ❏ 1 cup cocoa powder
- ❏ ¾ teaspoon salt
- ❏ ½ teaspoon cinnamon
- ❏ ½ teaspoon baking powder
- ❏ ½ cup plus 2 tablespoons unsalted butter, softened
- ❏ 1 cup light brown sugar, packed
- ❏ 1 large egg
- ❏ ½ cup whole milk
- ❏ 2 teaspoons vanilla extract
- ❏ 10 strawberry or other flavored marshmallows, cut in half with kitchen shears or scissors

Icing:
- ❏ 3 cups confectioners' sugar
- ❏ ⅓ cup cocoa powder
- ❏ ½ cup sour cream

1. Heat the oven to 350°. In a medium bowl, sift together the flour, cocoa powder, salt, cinnamon, and baking powder and set aside.

2. Using an electric mixer set on medium-high speed, cream all the butter and brown sugar until fluffy, about 3 minutes. Add the egg and beat until mixed, about 1 minute. Combine the milk and vanilla. Turn the mixer to low speed and add half the milk mixture. Slowly add half the flour mixture, then the remaining milk mixture, then the remaining flour mixture. Mix until well blended, about 1 minute.

3. Line a cookie sheet with parchment paper. Using a 2-tablespoon scoop, drop balls of the dough onto the sheet, leaving about 3 inches between them. Bake for 10 minutes. Remove the cookies from the oven and top each with a halved marshmallow, cut side down, pressing it into the dough. Bake for an additional 4 minutes, then cool the cookies on a rack.

4. Make the icing: sift the confectioners' sugar and cocoa powder in a large bowl. Stir in the sour cream until it's smooth. Top the cookies with the icing so that the marshmallow is completely covered. Allow the icing to set, about 1 hour, before serving.

chocolate granola clusters

MAKES: 2 DOZEN | **PREP TIME:** 15 MINUTES | **CHILL TIME:** 3 HOURS

This old-time recipe makes a great primer for young holiday-cookie makers, since there's no baking involved. Instead, the chocolate coating is simmered on the stovetop and then stirred into the granola to create melt-in-your-mouth morsels.

INGREDIENTS

- ❑ 2 cups granola
- ❑ ¼ cup milk
- ❑ 4 tablespoons butter
- ❑ ⅓ cup sugar
- ❑ ¼ cup chocolate chips
- ❑ ¼ cup peanut butter
- ❑ ½ teaspoon vanilla extract
- ❑ Yogurt-covered raisins or peanuts

1. Have your child measure the granola into a large mixing bowl and then break up any clusters into small pieces with his fingers. Line a large baking sheet with waxed paper.

2. Warm the milk and butter in a medium saucepan over medium heat. When the butter is mostly melted, use a long-handled wooden spoon to stir in the sugar and chocolate chips. Continue to carefully stir the mixture until it comes to a boil, then quickly reduce the heat and cook the sauce at a low boil for 1 minute. Remove the pan from the heat and stir in the peanut butter and vanilla extract until smooth.

3. Immediately pour the sauce over the granola and stir well. Scoop mounded tablespoons of the mixture onto the lined baking sheet, leaving a little space between each one. Gently press a yogurt-covered raisin or peanut into each mound. Once the cookies have cooled completely, cover them with plastic wrap and refrigerate them for at least 3 hours before serving.

TIP: Make sure the pieces of granola are well coated with chocolate so the cookies hold together when you spoon the batter onto the baking sheet.

chocolate cherry mice

MAKES: 24 | **PREP TIME:** 45 MINUTES | **CHILL TIME:** 10 MINUTES

For a really special gift, package these little guys with a mouse-related holiday book, such as *The Night Before Christmas*, *How the Grinch Stole Christmas!*, or *The Nutcracker*.

INGREDIENTS

❑ 24 maraschino cherries with stems

❑ ¾ cup semisweet chocolate chips

❑ 24 milk chocolate Hershey's Kisses, unwrapped

❑ 48 almond slices

Icing:

❑ 1 cup confectioners' sugar

❑ Black paste food coloring

❑ Red food coloring

1. Drain the cherries and pat them dry with paper towels. Line a cookie sheet with waxed paper.

2. Place the chocolate chips in a microwave-safe bowl and heat them until smooth, working in 15-second intervals, stirring between each.

3. Holding a cherry by its stem, dip it into the chocolate and swirl it around to completely cover the fruit. Set it on its side on the waxed paper and immediately press a Hershey's Kiss onto the cherry for the head. For the ears, gently wedge two almond slices between the Kiss and the cherry. Repeat to make 24 mice.

4. Make a thick icing by mixing 1 cup of confectioners' sugar with a teaspoon of water. If the mixture is too dry, stir in more water, a few drops at a time, until you have a thick, smooth icing. Divide the icing among three small bowls.

5. Tint one bowl of icing black and one pink. Spoon each of the three icings into a plastic bag and snip a tiny corner from each. Pipe white eye dots on the mice, then refrigerate them until set, about 10 minutes. Add black pupils and pink noses. Keep the mice in the fridge until you're ready to serve them or give them away.

molasses gingersnaps
· ·

MAKES: 2 DOZEN | **PREP TIME:** 20 MINUTES | **BAKE TIME:** 8–9 MINUTES PER BATCH

Make yummy memories a part of your family by filling an old-fashioned cookie tin with these delectable holiday treats.

INGREDIENTS
- ❏ ¾ cup vegetable shortening
- ❏ 1 cup packed light brown sugar
- ❏ ¼ cup molasses
- ❏ 1 large egg
- ❏ 2 cups all-purpose flour
- ❏ 2 teaspoons baking soda
- ❏ ¼ teaspoon salt
- ❏ 1 teaspoon ground cinnamon
- ❏ 1 teaspoon ground cloves
- ❏ 1 teaspoon ground ginger
- ❏ ½ cup sugar

1. In a large mixing bowl, cream together the shortening, brown sugar, molasses, and egg.

2. In a separate medium-size bowl, sift together the flour, baking soda, salt, and spices. Gradually add the dry ingredients to the creamed mixture, blending after each addition, until the dough is evenly mixed.

3. Heat the oven to 375°. Put the ½ cup of sugar in a medium-size bowl. Using floured hands, shape the dough into balls the size of whole walnuts. Roll the balls in the sugar, then place them on a large, lightly greased baking sheet, leaving a couple of inches between them. Bake for 8 to 9 minutes.

4. Cool the cookies on the baking sheet for 1 minute before transferring them to a cooling rack.

gingerbread family kit

MAKES: 18–20 5-INCH COOKIES | **PREP TIME:** 40 MINUTES | **CHILL TIME:** 1–2 HOURS | **BAKE TIME:** ABOUT 10 MINUTES

This kit of baked gingerbread men, decorators' frosting, and candies will give a family all the pleasures of cookie decorating without having to bake.

INGREDIENTS

- ❏ 4½ cups all-purpose flour
- ❏ 1 tablespoon cinnamon
- ❏ 2 teaspoons ground ginger
- ❏ 1¼ teaspoons baking soda
- ❏ ½ cup butter, room temperature
- ❏ ½ cup packed brown sugar
- ❏ 2 eggs
- ❏ ¾ cup molasses
- ❏ Kit supplies: white decorators' frosting, M&M's Minis, cinnamon Red Hots, tissue paper, plastic containers, shoestring licorice

1. In a large mixing bowl, combine the flour, cinnamon, ginger, and baking soda.

2. In a separate large bowl, cream the butter and brown sugar with an electric mixer. Add the eggs one at a time, then beat in the molasses. Slowly add the dry ingredients, beating after each addition (the dough will become quite stiff).

3. Divide the dough in half, shape into disks, and wrap in plastic. Chill for 1 to 2 hours or until the dough is firm enough to roll.

4. Heat the oven to 350°. On a lightly floured surface, roll out one piece of dough to a ⅛- to ¼-inch thickness. Use a 5-inch gingerbread person cookie cutter to cut the dough and use a spatula to transfer the gingerbread people to an ungreased baking sheet.

5. Bake for 10 minutes or until the cookies are lightly browned. Cool thoroughly. Repeat the process with the remaining dough.

6. To assemble a kit, line a 9-inch square plastic container with decorative tissue paper, add about 4 undecorated cookies, candies for decorating the cookies, and a tube of frosting. Design a label to affix to the lid. Makes 4 to 5 kits.

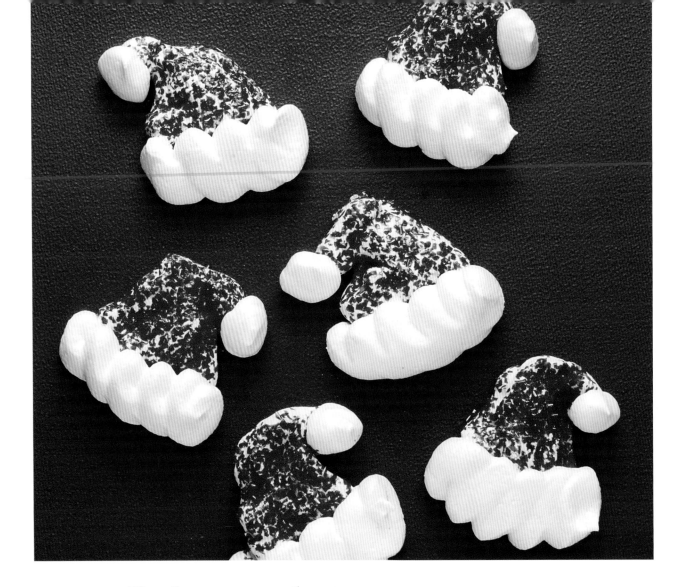

sweet little santa hats

MAKES: 24 HATS | **PREP TIME:** 30 MINUTES | **BAKE TIME:** 80 MINUTES

When it comes to classroom treats, our crispy meringue confections aren't easy to top: they're brimming with kid appeal, and a single recipe makes a big batch.

INGREDIENTS

- ❏ 2 egg whites, at room temperature
- ❏ ½ teaspoon cream of tartar
- ❏ ¼ teaspoon vanilla extract
- ❏ ½ cup sugar
- ❏ Red-colored sugar

1. Heat the oven to 200°. With an electric mixer set on medium speed, beat the egg whites until soft peaks start to form. Beating all the while, add the cream of tartar and the vanilla extract, then slowly add the white sugar. Continue to beat until stiff peaks form.

2. Spoon the meringue into a quart-size plastic bag and snip a corner from the bag. On a parchment-lined baking sheet, pipe 24 (1½-inch-long) Santa-hat triangles; you should have about a quarter of the meringue left. Sprinkle the triangles with the red sugar, then use the remaining meringue to give each one a pom-pom and trim.

3. Bake the hats until they're hard but not browned, about 1 hour and 20 minutes. Turn off the oven and leave the hats in it for an hour to crisp before removing them.

orange cornmeal crisps

MAKES: 48 COOKIES | **PREP TIME:** 30 MINUTES | **CHILL TIME:** 1 HOUR | **BAKE TIME:** 10-12 MINUTES PER BATCH

Citrus tang and cornmeal crunch make these crisps stand out on a holiday cookie platter. If blood oranges are available, use them to lend a rosier hue to the glaze.

INGREDIENTS

Cookies:

❑ 2 cups flour

❑ 1 cup fine cornmeal, divided

❑ 2 teaspoons baking powder

❑ ¼ teaspoon salt

❑ 1 cup unsalted butter, softened

❑ 1 cup sugar

❑ 1 large egg

❑ 1 to 2 teaspoons orange zest

❑ ½ teaspoon orange extract

Glaze:

❑ 2 cups confectioners' sugar, sifted

❑ Zest and juice of 2 medium oranges

❑ Pinch of fine sea salt

1. In a medium bowl, whisk together the flour, ¾ cup of the cornmeal, the baking powder, and salt, then set the mixture aside.

2. Using an electric mixer set on medium speed, beat the butter, sugar, and egg until creamy (scraping the bowl often), about 2 minutes. Reduce the speed to low; add the flour mixture, zest, and orange extract, and beat until the mixture pulls away from the sides and forms a dough, about 1 minute.

3. Divide the dough in half and form each half into a 12-inch-long, 1½-inch-wide log. Cover the dough in plastic wrap and chill until firm, about 1 hour in the refrigerator or 20 minutes in the freezer.

4. Heat the oven to 375°. Line two rimmed cookie sheets with parchment paper. Spread the remaining ¼ cup cornmeal on a small flat tray; roll each log in the cornmeal to coat. Cut the logs into ½-inch-thick slices and place them 1 inch apart on the prepared sheets. Bake until the cookies are deep golden brown around the edges, about 10 to 12 minutes, rotating the sheets halfway through. Cool the trays on a wire rack for about 5 minutes, then transfer the cookies to the rack to continue cooling.

5. To make the glaze, stir together the confectioners' sugar, zest, ¼ cup of the orange juice, and the salt. If needed, add more juice, a teaspoon at a time, until the glaze has a flowing consistency. Spoon a few teaspoons of the glaze onto each cookie.

the elves' snickerdoodles

MAKES: ABOUT 24 COOKIES | **PREP TIME:** 30 MINUTES | **CHILL TIME:** 30–60 MINUTES | **BAKE TIME:** 15–18 MINUTES PER BATCH

"Santa's baker elves know that one sure way to keep us elves happy is by serving plenty of these sparkly sugar-topped Snickerdoodles. The name alone just gives us the giggles."—One of Santa's elves

INGREDIENTS

- ❏ 2¼ cups flour
- ❏ ½ teaspoon baking powder
- ❏ ½ teaspoon baking soda
- ❏ ½ teaspoon salt
- ❏ ¼ teaspoon ground nutmeg
- ❏ ½ cup vegetable shortening
- ❏ 2 tablespoons soft butter
- ❏ 1 cup sugar
- ❏ 1 large egg
- ❏ ⅓ cup sour cream
- ❏ 1 teaspoon vanilla extract
- ❏ 1 teaspoon grated lemon zest
- ❏ Colored sugar or edible glitter

1. Sift the flour, baking powder, baking soda, salt, and nutmeg into a large mixing bowl. In a separate bowl, using an electric mixer, cream the shortening and butter. Gradually mix in the sugar. Beat in the egg until blended, then the sour cream, vanilla extract, and lemon zest.

2. With a wooden spoon, stir the dry ingredients into the creamed mixture half at a time, until evenly mixed. Cover the dough with plastic wrap and refrigerate it for 30 to 60 minutes.

3. Shortly before baking, heat the oven to 350°. Lightly grease 1 or 2 large cookie sheets, or line them with parchment paper. Put the decorative sugar into small bowls.

4. With lightly floured hands, shape the dough into 1½-inch balls. Roll the balls in the colored sugar and place them on the prepared baking sheets spaced about 3 inches apart. Bake the cookies on the center oven rack for 15 to 18 minutes, until they're a light golden brown. Cool the cookies on the sheet for 2 or 3 minutes. Use a spatula to transfer them to a wire rack to finish cooling.

baked snowflakes

· ·

MAKES: 6 | **PREP TIME:** 10 MINUTES | **BAKE TIME:** 4–6 MINUTES

Santa would be pleasantly surprised to find this sweet and crispy treat on his snack plate. It's simple enough to bake right before bedtime.

INGREDIENTS

❑ 6 flour tortillas
❑ Canola or vegetable
   oil for baking
❑ Confectioners' sugar
❑ Edible glitter (optional)

1. Heat the oven to 400°. Warm the tortillas (about 15 seconds) in the microwave. Fold each tortilla in half once and then in half again, to form a thick pie wedge. Use clean scissors to snip shapes from the edges of each wedge as if you were making paper snowflakes, then unfold them.

2. Lightly brush the tops of the tortillas with canola or vegetable oil and place them on a cookie sheet, leaving space between them. Bake the tortillas until lightly browned and crisp, about 4 to 6 minutes. Sift confectioners' sugar on the snowflakes while they're warm. For an extra sparkly effect, sprinkle on a bit of edible glitter.

sweet macaroon angels

MAKES: 12 | PREP TIME: 40 MINUTES | BAKE TIME: 20-25 MINUTES

These little angels make a heavenly holiday treat. The secret is mixing two kinds of coconut for the best flavor and consistency: the flaked, sweetened kind and the shredded, unsweetened variety.

INGREDIENTS:

- ❏ 1¼ cups sweetened flaked coconut
- ❏ 1¼ cups unsweetened shredded coconut
- ❏ ½ cup sugar
- ❏ 1½ tablespoons flour
- ❏ ⅛ teaspoon salt
- ❏ 2 large egg whites
- ❏ 1½ teaspoons honey
- ❏ ½ teaspoon vanilla extract
- ❏ 36 Necco wafers

1. With clean, dry hands, thoroughly combine the two types of coconut in a large bowl.

2. In a medium-size bowl, combine the sugar, flour, and salt. Add the egg whites, honey, and vanilla extract and rapidly whisk the batter until smooth and frothy, about 30 seconds.

3. Pour the mixture over the coconut and toss with a fork, then use a wooden spoon to continue mixing until the coconut is evenly coated. Cover the bowl with plastic wrap and refrigerate it for 30 minutes.

4. Heat the oven to 300° and line a large baking sheet with parchment paper or aluminum foil lightly coated with cooking spray. Place 12 evenly spaced mounds of dough on the baking sheet, each about ¼ cup, loosely packed. With your hands, gently shape each mound into a tall cone with a blunt top. If the dough sticks to your fingers, dampen them with water, shake off the excess, then continue.

5. Bake the macaroons on the center oven rack until they're light golden brown, about 20 to 25 minutes. Cool them for about 5 minutes on the baking sheet, then transfer them to a wire rack to cool for several hours.

6. Make a slot for the candy wings and head by using a sharp serrated knife to saw a groove partway down the cone (a parent's job). Once you've started the cut, lightly pinch together the sides of the cookie to keep it from crumbling as you slice.

7. Insert two Necco wafers into the sides of the groove for the wings, and wedge a third in the top for the angel's head. Gently press the macaroon back together to secure the wafers.

merry meringue treats

MAKES: 20 TREATS | **PREP TIME:** 30 | **BAKE TIME:** 10–12 MINTUES PER BATCH

Based on a popular french pastry called a macaroon, these tiny treats consist of two meringue cookies joined by a sweet filling. Enjoy a tasty tribute to the season.

INGREDIENTS

Vanilla Cookies:
- ❏ 2 large eggs
- ❏ 1 cup sifted almond flour or meal (found in the baking section of some supermarkets or at natural food stores)
- ❏ 1¼ cups confectioners' sugar
- ❏ ⅛ teaspoon salt
- ❏ ¼ cup sugar

Buttercream:
- ❏ 2 tablespoons butter, melted
- ❏ 2 tablespoons milk
- ❏ 1 teaspoon vanilla extract
- ❏ 1 cup confectioners' sugar

1. Line two cookie sheets with parchment paper and set them aside. Tip: Use a dab of water, oil, or butter to secure the paper to the pans.

2. Over a small bowl, separate the egg whites from the yolks. If any yolk slips into the bowl, scoop it out with an eggshell half so that the whites will beat properly. Discard the yolks. Let the whites sit at room temperature for 30 minutes.

3. Sift together the almond flour or meal and the confectioners' sugar into a medium-size mixing bowl. In a second bowl, using an electric mixer set on medium speed, beat together the egg whites and the salt until foamy, about 2 minutes. Increase the mixer's speed to high and gradually add the sugar. Continue to beat until stiff, glossy peaks form, about 1 minute more.

4. Gently fold the egg whites into the almond mixture with a rubber spatula, being careful not to deflate the meringue.

5. Place some of the meringue in a pastry bag fitted with a ³⁄₈-inch round tip, or a ziplock plastic bag with a corner snipped. Beginning at the corner of one cookie sheet and holding the bag perpendicular to the sheet's surface, squeeze out enough meringue to make a 1-inch disk. Pull the tip away from the disk with a quick circular motion to avoid making a peak (a misshapen cookie can be gently molded with a wet finger). Continue piping the cookies, spacing them 2 inches apart and refilling the bag as needed, until all the meringue is used.

6. Gently tap the bottom of each cookie sheet against the countertop to further flatten the cookies (they should be about ¼-inch thick), then allow them to sit at room temperature until dry to the touch, about 1½ hours.

7. Heat the oven to 325°. Bake the cookies, one pan at a time, in the center of the oven for 10 to 12 minutes. Allow each pan to cool on a wire rack.

8. Whisk together all the ingredients for the buttercream in a medium-size bowl until the mixture is smooth and shiny. Fill a clean pastry bag with the buttercream (alternatively, use a snipped plastic bag, or a butter knife or spatula).

9. Pair similar-size cookies. Pipe or spread a dollop of the buttercream on the flat side of one from each pair, then sandwich the pairs together.

holiday wreaths

MAKES: 4 DOZEN | **PREP TIME:** 30 MINUTES | **BAKE TIME:** 7–9 MINUTES PER BATCH

These buttery wreaths are more often called Spritz Cookies because they are squirted through a cookie press. If you don't own a cookie press, use a pastry bag fitted with a star-shaped tip (bags and tips are available at kitchen and party supply stores).

INGREDIENTS

- ❏ 1 cup (2 sticks) unsalted butter, softened
- ❏ ⅔ cup granulated sugar
- ❏ 2 large egg yolks
- ❏ ½ teaspoon almond extract
- ❏ 2¼ cups all-purpose flour
- ❏ Green sprinkles
- ❏ Red hots

1. Heat the oven to 375°. In a large mixing bowl, use a wooden spoon to cream the butter and sugar together until smooth. Stir in the egg yolks and almond extract. Gradually stir in the flour.

2. Assemble the cookie press and fit it with the star-shaped plate. Alternatively, fit a pastry bag with a star tip. Spoon the prepared dough into the press or bag and check the consistency of the dough with a test squeeze. If the dough is too soft, place the press or bag and remaining dough in the refrigerator to make it firmer. (Keep in mind that the consistency of the dough as it is squeezed through the press affects the look of the wreaths. If it is firmer, it is a little more difficult to press but gives a more jagged, leafy look to the wreaths. If the dough is warmer and softer, you will create smoother ridges.)

3. Working on an ungreased baking sheet, pipe the dough into circles to make wreaths, leaving 1 inch between the cookies. Decorate the cookies with green sprinkles and garnish each one with 3 red hots (you can use the candies to cover the spot where the circle joins). Bake the cookies for 7 to 9 minutes or until lightly browned.

4. Cool on the baking sheets for about 5 minutes. Using a metal spatula, transfer the cookies to a wire rack to cool completely. Repeat until all the dough is used.

jolly jelly thumbprints

MAKES: 4 DOZEN | **PREP TIME:** 30 MINUTES | **CHILL TIME:** 1–2 HOURS | **BAKE TIME:** 10–12 MINUTES PER BATCH

With these jelly-filled cookies, even very young chefs can make their mark on cookie dough. For other filling options, try pressing a few chocolate chips, M&M's, or a chocolate kiss into the just-baked cookies.

INGREDIENTS

- ❑ 1 cup (2 sticks) unsalted butter, softened
- ❑ ½ cup firmly packed brown sugar
- ❑ 1 large egg
- ❑ 1 teaspoon vanilla extract
- ❑ 3 cups all-purpose flour
- ❑ ½ cup teaspoon salt
- ❑ Granulated sugar (for rolling cookies)
- ❑ About ½ cup jelly or preserves

1. In a large mixing bowl, using a wooden spoon, cream the butter and brown sugar together until smooth. Stir in the egg and vanilla extract until combined. Gradually stir in the flour and salt. Cover the dough and refrigerate it for at least 1 to 2 hours or until the dough is firm enough to roll into balls.

2. Heat the oven to 350°. Form scant tablespoonfuls of the dough into 1-inch balls. Roll the balls in a bowl of granulated sugar. Place the balls on an ungreased baking sheet, leaving 2 inches between them.

3. Using your thumb, your knuckle, or the end of a wooden spoon, press an indentation into the center of each cookie. If the cookie cracks, press the crack together to make it smooth. Fill the center of each cookie with about ½ teaspoon of jelly. Bake for 10 to 12 minutes or until lightly browned.

4. Cool on the baking sheets for about 2 minutes, then transfer to a wire rack to cool completely. Repeat until all the dough is used. These cookies can be stored in an airtight container at room temperature for 1 week.

sesame crisps

MAKES: 5 DOZEN | **PREP TIME:** 30 MINUTES | **BAKE TIME:** 10-12 MINUTES PER BATCH

These crunchy toasted-nut–flavored cookies pack up without crumbling. Send a dozen to a distant relative or bring a batch along on your holiday house visits.

INGREDIENTS

- ❑ 1 cup sesame seeds
- ❑ ½ cup butter
- ❑ ½ cup white sugar
- ❑ ½ cup brown sugar
- ❑ 1 egg
- ❑ 1 teaspoon vanilla extract
- ❑ 1¼ cups flour
- ❑ ½ teaspoon baking powder
- ❑ ¼ teaspoon cinnamon
- ❑ ¼ teaspoon nutmeg
- ❑ ¼ teaspoon salt

1. Heat the oven to 350°. Toast the sesame seeds on a baking sheet for about 10 minutes, stirring occasionally to keep them from burning. Set the seeds aside to cool thoroughly.

2. In a mixing bowl, cream together the butter and sugars. Beat in the egg and vanilla extract. Add the flour, baking powder, cinnamon, nutmeg, and salt, mixing until thoroughly combined. Fold in ¹/₃ cup of the sesame seeds. Shape the dough into ¾-inch balls and roll them in the remaining sesame seeds to coat the surface of each one. Place the balls on two greased cookie sheets, leaving at least 1 inch between them, and bake until golden brown, about 10 to 12 minutes. Allow the cookies to cool on the sheets for 2 minutes, then use a spatula to transfer them to a wire rack.

raspberry tarts

MAKES: ABOUT 26 | **PREP TIME:** 40 MINUTES | **BAKE TIME:** 10 MINUTES PER BATCH

Share a little holiday love and sweetness with raspberry-jam-filled heart-shaped tarts.

INGREDIENTS

- ❏ 3 cups all-purpose flour
- ❏ 5 egg yolks
- ❏ 1 cup butter, softened
- ❏ ½ cup plus 2 tablespoons sugar
- ❏ ½ teaspoon vanilla extract
- ❏ 2 egg whites, lightly beaten
- ❏ ⅓ cup ground walnuts
- ❏ 1½ cups seedless raspberry jam

1. In a large bowl, mix the flour, egg yolks, butter, ½ cup sugar, and vanilla extract, then knead until it forms a soft dough. Chill for 30 minutes.

2. On a floured surface, roll the dough ⅛-inch thick. Cut a heart for the bottom of the cookie sandwich, and a heart with a smaller heart cut in it for the top. Brush the tops with egg whites.

3. Mix the walnuts with the 2 tablespoons of sugar and sprinkle on the cookie tops. Place on an ungreased cookie sheet and bake in an oven preheated to 350° for 10 minutes. Cool.

4. Spread the bottom hearts with a layer of jam and put the tops on.

a light dessert

PREP TIME: 6 MINUTES EACH

These festive treats can brighten any holiday gathering, from Hanukkah to New Year's and all the celebrations in between.

1. Make a simple icing by stirring together 1 teaspoon water and 5 tablespoons confectioners' sugar.

2. Use dots of icing to attach a small flower cookie with a center hole (we used Murray shortbread cookies) to a larger cookie (we used Anna's Ginger Thins). Dab icing on one end of a rolled wafer cookie (we used Pepperidge Farm Pirouettes) and press it into the center of the flower cookie.

3. For the flame, halve a mini marshmallow diagonally, dip the sticky side of one half in orange decorating sugar, and attach the half with icing. Spoon a few wax drips of icing down the candle's sides and use red decorating gel to embellish the base.

almond or chocolate shortbread cookies

MAKES: 4½ DOZEN COOKIES | **PREP TIME:** 30 MINUTES | **CHILL TIME:** 2 HOURS | **BAKE TIME:** 6–10 MINUTES PER BATCH

Nothing says old-fashioned goodness and tradition like shortbread cookies—the perfect treats with a spot of Christmas tea!

INGREDIENTS

- ❏ 1 cup unsalted butter, at room temperature
- ❏ ¾ cup confectioners' sugar, sifted
- ❏ ⅓ cup ground, blanched almonds, or ⅓ cup unsweetened cocoa powder
- ❏ ¼ teaspoon salt
- ❏ 2 cups all-purpose flour, sifted
- ❏ 1 egg white (optional)
- ❏ ¼ cup chopped almonds (optional)

1. Cream together with a mixer the butter, sugar, ground almonds (or cocoa powder), and salt. Add the flour, mixing just until incorporated.

2. Divide the dough into thirds and roll into 2-inch-wide logs on a sheet of waxed paper. Seal each log in plastic wrap, then store in the refrigerator for two hours or freeze for easier handling. If you prefer, you can roll out the dough and store it in ¼-inch-thick sheets, which is easier if you're using cookie cutters.

3. Slice ¼-inch-thick rounds from the dough logs, and place onto lightly-greased or parchment-paper-lined cookie sheets, one inch apart. Bake for 6–10 minutes, or until they are firm but not brown. If you're using frozen dough, the cookies may need more time to bake; check them after 8 minutes.

4. If desired, a few minutes before the cookies are done, remove them from the oven, brush with the egg white, top with chopped nuts, and resume baking.

snowballs

MAKES: ABOUT 4 DOZEN | **PREP TIME:** 20 MINUTES | **BAKE TIME:** 10 MINUTES PER BATCH

These are the perfect bite-size cookies to serve at any holiday gathering. Plus, they're simply finger-licking fun to eat!

INGREDIENTS

- ❏ 1 cup walnuts
- ❏ 1 cup margarine or butter, softened
- ❏ ½ cup confectioners' sugar
- ❏ 1 teaspoon vanilla extract or maple syrup
- ❏ 2¼ cups all-purpose flour
- ❏ ¼ teaspoon salt
- ❏ Confectioners' sugar, to cover

1. Finely chop the walnuts in a blender or food processor, then set aside. Cream together the margarine and ½ cup confectioners' sugar. Add the vanilla extract or syrup. Stir in the flour, salt, and walnuts.

2. Roll the dough into 1-inch balls and place them an inch apart on an ungreased cookie sheet. Bake in a preheated 400° oven until set but not brown (about 10 minutes).

3. Roll the cookies in confectioners' sugar while warm and then again when they've cooled.

peanut butter blossoms

MAKES: 37 COOKIES | **PREP TIME:** 20 MINUTES | **BAKE TIME:** 8, 3 MINUTES PER BATCH

INGREDIENTS

- ❏ ½ cup creamy peanut butter
- ❏ ½ cup sugar
- ❏ ½ cup butter, room temperature
- ❏ ½ cup firmly packed brown sugar
- ❏ 1 egg
- ❏ 1 teaspoon vanilla extract
- ❏ ½ teaspoon salt
- ❏ 1 teaspoon baking soda
- ❏ 1¾ cups all-purpose flour
- ❏ 1 (9-ounce) package chocolate Hershey Kisses

1. Preheat the oven to 375°. Cream the peanut butter, sugar, butter, and brown sugar. Add the egg and vanilla extract.

2. Sift the salt, baking soda, and flour together. Combine with the wet mixture. Shape into balls; dip in additional white sugar.

3. Bake 8 minutes, remove from oven, and press a chocolate kiss into each. Return to oven; bake another 3 minutes.

graham cracker chalet

MAKES: 1 HOUSE

As any builder will tell you, gingerbread house construction is traditionally tricky. But not so with this Alpine chalet. Made from a revolutionary new building material—graham crackers—it's a cinch for even first-time home builders.

YOU WILL NEED

- ❑ Craft knife and scissors
- ❑ Cardboard six-pack container
- ❑ Masking tape
- ❑ Yellow cellophane
- ❑ Small flashlight (3–4 inches)
- ❑ Corrugated cardboard
- ❑ Frosting
- ❑ Graham crackers
- ❑ Pretzel nibs, wafers, and assorted candies for decorating (see page 31)
- ❑ Golden Grahams cereal

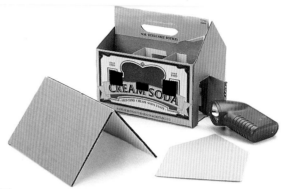

BASIC STRUCTURE

Using a craft knife (a parent's job), cut out windows on the long sides of the six-pack. Tape a square of cellophane inside each window. From one of the short sides, cut out a door to one side of the center seam. To make sure the flashlight will fit inside, try putting it through this door (cut out some of the inner structure so you can center the flashlight). Using the six-pack as a guide, outline and cut out of the corrugated cardboard a peaked wall for each short side (see above). From one peaked wall, cut out a hinged door in the same place as the one on the container. Tape both cardboard walls in place. Cut out a 12- by 9-inch piece of cardboard, then score and fold it in half for the roof. Lay it on top of the container, trimming if necessary, and tape in place.

SIDING

Starting at the front of the house and ending with the roof, apply icing to each surface using a butter knife, then press on graham crackers. **TIP:** Resize any crackers that don't fit by nibbling!

TRIM

Now you can decorate your house however you like, using icing to affix the decorations. We used rows of pretzel nibs and wafer cookies on the walls, accented with mini marshmallows and licorice-twist trim.

ROOF

Cover one side of the roof with icing. Apply the bottommost row of Golden Grahams, then overlap each successive layer, working upward. Repeat for the other side. Add a licorice ridgepole. For the chimney base, cut 2 Starburst candies in half diagonally and attach them to the roof with icing mortar. Top with more Starburst bricks. For white icicles, use clean scissors to cut long, thin triangles from large marshmallows. Attach these along the eaves with icing.

FINAL TOUCHES

Add any other decorations you like, such as starlight mint ornaments, a LifeSavers wreath, or confectioners' sugar snow. Allow all frosting to dry, then turn on the flashlight and slide it inside the house. Sweet!

HOME SWEET HOME

For more exterior decorating of your chalet, try the ideas below—or head to the candy aisle and dream up your own.

GUMDROPS: Set these out as boulders and shrubs or join with pretzel sticks to make a low fence. Or, use them as the heads and bodies of penguins and skiers (for the skiers, attach licorice limbs with toothpicks).

RED HOTS CANDIES: Perfect for tree decorations, holly berries, and house trim.

CARAMELS: Use these as stepping-stones or stack them up to make a stovepipe. You can also put two atop stacked chocolate wafer cookies for a moose's head. (Toothpicks make great spindly legs, use twist pretzels for antlers, and circus peanuts are great hooves.)

FRUIT ROLL-UP: Roll this out as a pathway or pond, or cut it to make flags and banners.

STARBURST FRUIT CHEWS: Great for brick paths, fences, or wishing wells.

PRETZEL STICKS: Pile up as firewood or use for fencing, roofing, or siding.

KIT KATS: Use these for a bench or skis.

LICORICE LACE: Outline doors and windows or string up as holiday lights.

MARSHMALLOWS: Pile up a few as a snowbank, stack together three for a snowman, or use large and mini sizes for a little polar bear.

NECCO WAFERS: These colorful disks make great siding, roof tiles, flagstones, and penguin wings.

SKITTLES: Use these to make house trim, holiday lights, roof tiles, or doorknobs.

GRAHAM CRACKERS: Great for shutters, pathways, docks, and signs.

SUGAR CONES: Coat these with a thin layer of icing and roll in green sugar to make a pine tree.

JELLY BEANS: Great for snowman or penguin noses and skiers' hands and feet.

rudolph's festive oatmeal cookies

MAKES: 16–18 COOKIES | **PREP TIME:** 40 MINUTES | **BAKE TIME:** 13–15 MINUTES PER BATCH

The shiniest nose in the world won't do a reindeer any good if he runs out of energy halfway through his Christmas Eve trip around the world. That's why Rudolph likes these chewy concoctions made with nuts, white chocolate chips, cranberries, and his favorite healthy grain—oats.

INGREDIENTS

- ❑ 1½ cups flour
- ❑ 1 teaspoon baking powder
- ❑ ½ teaspoon baking soda
- ❑ ½ teaspoon salt
- ❑ ½ teaspoon cinnamon
- ❑ ⅛ teaspoon ground cloves
- ❑ 1 cup unsalted butter, softened
- ❑ 1 cup packed light brown sugar
- ❑ ½ cup sugar
- ❑ 1 large egg
- ❑ 1½ teaspoons vanilla extract
- ❑ 3 cups uncooked oats, quick or old-fashioned
- ❑ ½ cup chopped walnuts or pecans
- ❑ ½ cup sweetened dried cranberries (such as Craisins)
- ❑ ½ cup white chocolate chips

1. Heat the oven to 350°. Grease 2 large baking sheets or line them with parchment paper.

2. Sift the flour, baking powder, baking soda, salt, cinnamon, and cloves into a large mixing bowl. In a separate bowl, cream the butter with an electric mixer, gradually beating in the sugars on medium-high speed. Beat in the egg until evenly blended, then the vanilla extract.

3. Stir the flour mixture into the creamed ingredients with a wooden spoon until well blended. Stir in the oats, nuts, dried cranberries, and white chocolate chips.

4. Drop 1 level quarter-cup of dough per cookie onto the baking sheets, leaving about 3½ inches between mounds. Bake the cookies, 1 sheet at a time, for 13 to 15 minutes, until the tops are an even light golden brown and crusty to the touch. Do not overbake. Cool the cookies on the sheet for 2 minutes, then use a spatula to transfer them to a wire rack to cool thoroughly.